THE PERFECT STORM

WHITE STAR PUBLISHERS

CONTENTS

SEA'S FURY

page twenty

THE BRAVE SAILORS

page seventy-two

WAVES

page one hundred and fourteen

RIDING THE WAVES

page one hundred and forty

Project editor VALERIA MANFERTO DE FABIANIS

Text by ORNELLA D'ALESSIO

Editorial coordination GIADA FRANCIA • GIORGIA RAINERI

Graphic design MARINELLA DEBERNARDI

Graphic layout PAOLA PIACCO

INTRODUCTION

THE STORM IS LIFE, PURE ENERGY, MOVEMENT. IT'S A RESTLESS FORCE OF NATURE THAT EXPRESSES ITSELF IN DIFFERENT WAYS, EVOKING DIFFERENT STATES OF MIND. THE MOST OBVIOUS MOVEMENT OF THE OCEAN IS CONSTITUTED BY THE WAVES THAT BREAK IMPETUOUSLY ONTO THE COASTS, OR THAT FLING THEMSELVES ROARING AGAINST JETTIES, LIGHTHOUSES, OR BARRIERS. FOR THOUSANDS OF YEARS THE SEA HAS NEVER STOPPED. EACH DROP WITHIN IT IS IN MOVEMENT, WITHOUT RESPITE, FROM THE POLES TO THE EQUATOR, FROM THE MARIANA TRENCH TO THE AZORES, FROM THE PACIFIC TO THE ATLANTIC.

BREAKERS FORM UNDER THE ACTION OF THE WIND BLOWING ACROSS THE SURFACE OF THE WATER, EXERTING A PRESSURE UPON IT TO THE POINT OF MAKING THE WATER RISE. WHEN THE LIQUID MASS THAT HAS RISEN BECOMES TOO HEAVY, THE PRESSURE CEASES, AND THE MASS FALLS AGAIN, PUSHING UPWARD THE PARTICLES OF WATER THAT ARE NEARBY, IN A CONTINUING OSCILLATION THAT PROPAGATES TO IMMENSE DISTANCES.

BUT A WAVE IS NOT SEAWATER TRAVELING HORIZONTALLY, BECAUSE ITS MOVEMENT IS SOLELY VERTICAL, AND THE WATER MOLECULES, EVEN THOUGH TRANSMITTING THE ENERGY OF THRUST, ONLY ADVANCE BUT LITTLE. LEONARDO WAS THE FIRST TO UNDERSTAND HOW A WAVE'S HORIZONTAL MOVEMENT IS ILLUSORY, BY OBSERVING THE WIND AS IT BLOWS THROUGH GRAINS OF WHEAT IN A FIELD.

THEREFORE, THE WAVE IN A STORM IS NOT A MASS OF WATER TRAVELING ON THE OCEAN'S SURFACE, BUT IT IS THE TRANSFERRING OF ENERGY FROM THE WIND TO THE WATER. A MANIFESTATION OF OVERWHELMING POWER, AN UNSTOPPABLE AND UNIMAGINABLE FURY, UNLEASHED WITHOUT FOREWARNING. IT IS THIS SENSATION OF BEING EXPOSED TO AN IRRESISTIBLE FORCE THAT TAKES POSSESSION OF THOSE GOING BY SEA AND THAT, ALONG WITH THE COMPETITIVE SPIRIT, IS PRESENT DURING SOLITARY OCEAN CROSSINGS, THE MOST DIFFICULT AND DEMANDING. TO ACCOMPLISH THESE ENTERPRISES ONE NEEDS SKILL, TENACITY, AND COURAGE, ASSETS THAT MUST BE EVER CONSTANT IN ORDER TO FACE THE SEA AND THE STORMS THAT MAY ARISE.

IN A SOLITARY ATLANTIC CROSSING, ONE JOURNEYS FOR WEEKS IN CONDITIONS THAT ARE SOMETIMES ADVERSE, COMPLETELY ALONE, BRAVING TERRIBLE AND IMPETUOUS STORMS WITHOUT THE AID OF ANYONE ELSE, MEASURING ONESELF AGAINST SUSTAINED WINDS REACHING EVEN AS HIGH AS 48 KNOTS AND WITH WAVES AS HIGH AS WALLS.

1 ATLANTIC OCEAN, FRANCE – LIGHTHOUSE IN THE STORM. 2-3 PACIFIC OCEAN, CHILE – STORM OVER CAPE HORN.

4-5 ATLANTIC OCEAN – THE *FUJIFILM* MULTIHULL. 6-7 MEDITERRANEAN SEA, FRANCE – THE CASSIS LIGHTHOUSE.

ERRORS ARE NOT PERMITTED. THE OCEAN DOES NOT FORGIVE. MANY NAVIGATORS HAVE RISKED LIFE AND SHIP FOR A SUBMERGED WRECK THAT APPEARED SUDDENLY IN THE NIGHT, OR GOT CARRIED AWAY BY A GIGANTIC ROGUE WAVE. WE OFTEN HEAR TALES OF EXCEPTIONAL WAVES: ALREADY CONSIDERED COLOSSAL IN SIZE WHEN THEY REACH A HEIGHT OF 26 FT (8 M). EVEN IN THE OCEANS THAT ARE MOST FREQUENTLY STRUCK BY STORMS, THEY DO NOT EXCEED 50-60 FT (15-20 M). THEIR FORCE IS TERRIBLE. WHEN CURRENTS OF COLD AND HOT AIR MEET, VORTICES OF AIR AND WATER CAN FORM; THESE BECOME CYCLONES, WATERSPOUTS, TYPHOONS, OR HURRICANES.

FRIGHTFUL FURIES OVERWHELM THE SEAS, PROVOKING APPALLING DAMAGE. THE MOVEMENTS OF THE OCEANS ARE CAPABLE OF CREATING SERIOUS PROBLEMS FOR THE MOST MODERN TRANSATLANTIC SHIPS, AND WHEN BREAKING ON THE SHORES THEY CAN SHIFT HEAVY MASSES WEIGHING HUNDREDS OF TONS. THE RAGES OF THE SEA LINKED WITH TELLURIC MOVEMENTS OR SEISMIC UPHEAVALS CREATE GIGANTIC WAVES THAT STRIKE THE COASTS WITH AN AWESOME MIGHT. THE BREAKERS WITH THEIR PERENNIAL AND AGITATED MOTION POLISH THE PEBBLES, ROUNDING AND FLATTENING THE SEASHORE. WHEN THE WAVES BEAT AGAINST THE ROCKS, THEY SLOWLY EXFOLIATE THEM, AND WITH THEIR CONTINUAL EROSIVE ACTION THEY MODIFY THE COASTAL PROFILES, WHICH BECOME EVER MORE IRREGULAR. THUS THROUGH THE MILLENNIA, GROTTOES HAVE BEEN DUG OUT AND ENORMOUS GRANITE MASSES HAVE BEEN DETACHED FROM THE COAST.

THE SEA, AND ITS ENERGY, STILL REMAINS A STRANGER TO US, THOUGH OUR LIVES ARE CONNECTED TO ITS VIOLENT STORMS. IMMENSE WAVES, SUBMARINES UPWELLING, SOLITARY AND DESTRUCTIVE WAVES: THE TALES OF SAILORS FROM TIMES PAST ABOUND WITH DESCRIPTIONS OF TERRIBLE STORMS AND OF MONSTERS. LEGENDS THAT HAVE GIVEN RISE TO AN AMPLE AMOUNT OF LITERATURE, IN WHICH OCEANS ARE PERCEIVED AS INHOSPITABLE ENVIRONMENTS, FEARSOME AND FRIGHTFUL; SPACES TO BRAVE ONLY IF ARMED WITH THE LUST FOR ADVENTURE OR DRIVEN BY THE MOST EXTREME OF NECESSITIES. JUST THINK OF THE WHALERS AND THE

14-15 MEDITERRANEAN SEA, ITALY – SEA STORM AT CAMOGLI. 16-17 PACIFIC OCEAN, HAWAII, U.S. – GLIDING AMONG THE REEFS.

18-19 PACIFIC OCEAN, HAWAII, U.S. – WHITE HORSES OFF THE COAST OF MAUI.

LONG POLAR NIGHTS, OF THE EXPLORERS WHO SAILED FOR MONTHS TOWARD UNKNOWN LANDS, OF THE FISH-ERMEN WHO FOR CENTURIES HAVE BRAVED THE MOST VIOLENT OF STORMS IN ORDER TO RETURN WITH THEIR NETS FILLED. THIS COURAGE—WHICH IS NEVER IRRESPONSIBILITY—THESE EXHAUSTING EFFORTS, THESE INTER-MINABLY LONG DAYS WITH THE INFINITE EVER BEFORE THE EYES ARE SOMETHING POETIC. PERHAPS THE WHOLE THING CAN BE EXPLAINED BY THE STRONG DESIRE FOR REDEMPTION BLENDED WITH THE GREAT LOVE FOR THE NATURAL ELEMENT, ALMOST AS THOUGH IT WERE ONLY IN THE MIDST OF THE SEA THAT ONE CAN EXPERIENCE AND FIND AGAIN AN EQUILIBRIUM THAT BY NOW HAS VANISHED, A HUMANITY NEVER BEFORE EXPERIENCED, A DIMENSION NO LONGER UNDERSTOOD, PERHAPS LOST FOREVER.

THE FORCE, POWER, AND VIGOR OF THE OCEANS REMAIN EVEN WHEN THE WAVES APPEAR TO HAVE BECOME MORE DOCILE, ALLOWING THEMSELVES TO BE STRADDLED BY HARDY SURFERS WHO CHALLENGE THE FORCE OF GRAVITY WITH ACROBATICS AND SPECTACULAR BALANCING ACTS UPON THE CRESTS OF IMMENSE MASSES OF WATER SEVERAL YARDS HIGH. A GREAT SENSE OF ARTISTRY PERVADES THE MOVEMENTS OF SURFERS WHEN THEY UNHESITATINGLY VENTURE INTO A FIGHT WITH NATURE BY ATTACKING THE FRIGHTFUL POWER OF THE WAVES TO GOVERN THEM FOR THEIR PLEASURE, IN A TEST OF ATHLETICS EXPRESSED IN PERFECT SYMBIOSIS WITH THE WAVE, AND IN WHICH MAN AND NATURE COEXIST HARMONIOUSLY.

IT IS MARVELOUS TO WITNESS WINTER TEMPESTS AND SEA STORMS, WHEN THE FURY OF THE ELEMENTS CAN BE OBSERVED FROM ABOVE (A GOOD POINT OF VIEW), PERHAPS EVEN ALLOWING ONESELF TO BE CAR-RIED AWAY BY THE CHARM AND EXTRAORDINARY BEAUTY OF NATURE AS IT ROARS SO MIGHTILY. THIS TYPE OF SEA HAS INSPIRED ARTISTS, PAINTERS, AND MUSICIANS WHO HAVE TRANSLATED NATURE'S ENERGY INTO SO MANY MASTERPIECES; FOR EXAMPLE, *THE STORM AT SEA* FROM ANTONIO VIVALDI'S (1678-1741) FIFTH VIOLIN CONCERTO.

SEA'S FURY

"I don't believe I've ever seen anything so terrifying," wrote explorer Matthew Flinders after rounding Cape Otway, in Australia. Eighty shipwrecks and many hundreds of lives later, the gorgeous 81 miles (130 km) separating Moonlight Head from Port Fairy earned the title of "Shipwreck Coast." The constant physical, symbolic, and immense presence of the ocean. These are the "Roaring Forties" that beat ceaselessly onto this coast.

It is a sea to be feared, as hundreds of mariners have learned the hard way in the last 150 years. Off the coast from these cliffs passed the route for clippers headed for the ports of Sydney and Melbourne. The passage is obligatory, because Bass Strait is divided by King Island into two channels. The deadly reefs obstructing the southern arm left no alternative to captains of those times.

The storms, currents, and fogs, have exacted an extremely high toll through the years. Over 80 vessels have been wrecked along these sea cliffs. In following along the Historic Shipwreck Trail, which coincides with a tract of the Great Ocean Road, we come upon the skeletons of these watercrafts. What the sea has scattered on the beaches and what men have recovered. They're everywhere, you can see them as you stroll along the beaches, like the anchors of the Fiji, or hanging on walls in pubs and museums, or set up in the villages. The great wrecks are there, underwater, a veritable paradise for diving enthusiasts. Many have been identified and their treasures recovered. Others, like the mysterious *Mahogany*, continue to evade searchers.

THE PRINCIPLE OF TWO COMMUNICATING VESSELS SEEMS SIMPLE: A CERTAIN AMOUNT OF LIQUID GOES DOWN, AND SO MUCH GOES UP; WHAT IS EMPTIED, IMMEDIATELY AFTERWARD, GETS FILLED. IN PHYSICS, IT IS A TRIVIAL NOTION, BUT IN WEATHER, THE EFFECT CAN BE TERRIBLE. IT IS THE MOVEMENTS OF HOT AIR AND COLD AIR THAT CREATES THE DISTURBANCE WHEN THEY MEET, THE FORCE OF THE WIND, AND THEN THE STORM. THE SEA CHANGES APPEARANCE IN A FEW MOMENTS: IT RIPPLES THEN RISES, THE WAVES BECOME OVERPOWERING, THE CRESTS BREAK UP, AND THE WATER TURNS INTO SPRAY.

IF THE STORM ARRIVING IS A BAD ONE, THEN ALL HELL BREAKS LOOSE: THE FORCES OF THE SEA, OF THE WAVES, ESPECIALLY THOSE COMING FROM AFAR, ARE CHARGED WITH AN UNIMAGINABLE ENERGY. THEY CAN FLING THEMSELVES AGAINST THE COASTS AND PRACTICALLY ERASE THE WORLD. IN 2001, DURING A STORM THAT HIT THE COAST OF NORWAY, THE WAVES ROSE UP ALONG THE SEA CLIFFS OF THE ISLAND THAT HOSTS THE LIGHTHOUSE MARSTEIN. THE WAVES HURLED AGAINST THE GREAT WALL OF REINFORCED CEMENT, RIPPED OFF ENORMOUS BLOCKS, CARRIED AND HEAVED THEM AGAINST THE BUILDINGS, AS THOUGH THEY WERE GIGANTIC HANDS.

OFF THE COAST, YOU CAN LOSE YOUR HEAD. IT SEEMS LIKE THE WATER IS COMING FROM ALL DIRECTIONS, OVERWHELMING EVERYTHING, EVEN THE LUCIDITY OF ANYONE FINDING HIMSELF AT THE MERCY OF THE WAVES. BUT NOT ONLY THE WATER: THE HOWLING OF THE WIND CAN BE JUST AS TERRIBLE. WITH THE WIND AT 40 TO 50 KNOTS (ABOUT 60 MPH OR 90 KM/H) YOU CAN'T HEAR WHAT YOUR SAILING COMPANION IS TELLING YOU FROM A DISTANCE OF TWO METERS. ONE DAY IN 1805, A CERTAIN FRANCIS BEAUFORT, ADMIRAL OF THE BRITISH FLEET, CONCEIVED AN INTENSITY SCALE FOR ESTIMATING WIND SPEED

OVER THE SEA. THE SYSTEM ASSIGNS NAMES AND NUMBERS TO 12 DIFFERENT SITUATIONS, FROM CALM TO HURRICANE, FROM BREEZE TO STRONG GALE.

THIS IS STILL IN USE TODAY, BUT ITS VALUE IS ONLY INDICATIVE WHEN MORE PRECISE MEASURING INSTRUMENTS ARE NOT AVAILABLE. AT THE SEVENTH DEGREE ON THE SCALE, WE READ: "GALE. THE SEA BECOMES WHITE WITH FOAM, EVEN LARGER BOATS SEEK SHELTER. IN OPEN SEA, SAILS REDUCED TO THE MINIMUM, TAKE THE WIND FROM ASTERN, IF NECESSARY, WITH ONLY THE JIB." WORDS THAT CAN BE UNDERSTOOD BY SOMEONE IN THE MIDST OF A STORM, WHEN TO MAKE IT THROUGH YOU HAVE TO LET YOURSELF BE DRIVEN BY THE WIND, NEVER TO CONFRONT IT.

AN ADAGE SAYS THAT TO GOVERN THE FORCES OF NATURE, YOU HAVE TO SATISFY THEM. AT SEA, THIS IS RESOUNDINGLY TRUE. SPLENDID ARE THE IMAGES OF OCEANS IN STORMS, AND DELIGHTFUL MAY APPEAR THE COLORS OF THE AGITATED WATER, RENDERING THE BREAKERS FASCINATING AS THEY MIX WITH THE SUN'S RAYS...BUT THE VISION IS DIFFERENT WHEN YOU ARE SAILING AND FIND YOURSELF LITERALLY SURROUNDED BY THESE MONSTERS IN ETERNAL MOVEMENT.

STRIKING AND DRAMATIC ARE THE SHIP'S DIARIES FROM THE EARLY 1900S, WHERE THE MISADVENTURES, THE EFFORT, THE TERROR (AND ALSO THE MOURNING) ARE SO "HUMANLY" DESCRIBED THAT THEY ARE TOUCHING. MEN, IN SPITE OF THEMSELVES, COURAGEOUS IN THEIR FIGHT AGAINST THE WAVES THAT SUBMERGE THE HULL, AND ONLY THROUGH THEIR OWN SKILL ARE THEY ABLE TO SAVE THEMSELVES. POWERFUL TESTIMONIES THAT MAKE THE SEA APPEAR AN IMPLACABLE DEVOURER OF LIVES AND SHIPS, DESTROYER OF SAILS, AND, IN SOME CASES, ALSO OF HUMAN PERSONALITIES AND ESSENCES.

24-25 AND **26-27** MEDITERRANEAN SEA, ITALY – A VIOLENT SEA STORM OVERWHELMS THE CLIFFS OF CAMOGLI, IN LIGURIA.

28-29 SOUTHERN ATLANTIC OCEAN, FALKLAND ISLANDS – A FLOCK OF ALBATROSSES CHALLENGE THE TEMPEST.

"Do you not know how I love? I love the way the sea loves the shore: sweetly and furiously!"

Federico De Roberto

30-31 ATLANTIC OCEAN, FRANCE – WAVES BREAKING AGAINST THE LIGHTHOUSE AT SAINT-VALERY-EN-CAUX, A TOWN ON THE NORMANDY COAST.

32-33 Atlantic Ocean, Portugal – Compared to the waves crashing violently against the cliffs of the Algarve, the two fishermen appear small and fragile.

34-35 Southern Indian Ocean, Antarctica – A rookery of king penguins dash headlong to escape the storm raging on the beach.

36-37 Atlantic Ocean, France – A solitary seagull flies over a wall of foam generated by the sea storm.

38-39 Southern Indian Ocean, Antarctica – Beyond the handrail of a passenger ship, the hurricane manifests in all its violence.

40-41 Southern Indian Ocean, Antarctica – The sea in the tempest hurls itself against an iceberg off the shore of the South Orkney Islands.

42-43 Atlantic Ocean, North Sea – The agitated sea and the obscurity of the sky are harbingers of the storm about to fall upon the *Frigg* platform.

44-45 Atlantic Ocean – A violent storm classified as force 10 on the Beaufort scale distresses the ocean surface.

46-47 ATLANTIC OCEAN, GREAT BRITAIN – THE WAVES CREATED BY A WINTER STORM CRASH FORCEFULLY AGAINST THE CLIFFS OF CORNWALL.

48-49 ATLANTIC OCEAN, FRANCE – THE DIMINUTIVE LOMENER LIGHTHOUSE IN BRITTANY IS ISOLATED AMONG THE BREAKERS.

50-51 MEDITERRANEAN SEA, ITALY – WHIRLWINDS OFF THE COAST OF STROMBOLI CREATE A RARE AND MENACING WATERSPOUT.

"TODAY THE SEA PERFUMES THE ISLAND'S ROADS: THE NORTHWEST WIND OPENS THE PORES OF THE SKIN, WASHES THE FACES OF THE HOUSES, SPLITS THE WAVES AND THE COURSE. ON LAND, WAITING FOR THE FORCE OF THE WIND TO CONSUME ITSELF."

EMIL CIORAN, FROM CAHIERS ("NOTEBOOKS")

52-53 AND 54-55 ATLANTIC OCEAN, FRANCE — WINTER STORMS STRIKE
THE SMALL VILLAGE OF SAINT-GUÉNOLÉ IN BRITTANY WITH SUCH FORCE THAT
ITS VIBRATIONS CAN BE FELT MILES WAY.

56-57 Atlantic Ocean, France – The mighty sea storm threatens the port of Moëlan-sur-Mer, a small Breton town.

58-59 ATLANTIC OCEAN, FRANCE – GUSTS OF WIND AND FOAM ASSAIL THE PIERRES NOIRES LIGHTHOUSE, SITUATED ON A SMALL, ROCKY ISLAND OFF THE BRITTANY COAST.

60-61 PACIFIC OCEAN – DARK STORM CLOUDS LOOM IN VIVID CONTRAST TO THE MURKY COLOR OF THE WATER.

62-63 PACIFIC OCEAN, U.S. – DRIVEN BY THE FORCE OF THE WIND, HIGH ROLLERS BREAK AGAINST THE SHORE.

64-65 Pacific Ocean, Hawaii, U.S. – The typhoon's fury has lifted a watercraft and cast it on the shore.

THE BARRIER WE HAVE AGAINST
THE SEA IS UNDERMINED; THE
WATER OVERCOMES MYRIADS OF
PEBBLES; OUR DOORS ARE FILLED
WITH SAND AND STONES.

VICTOR HUGO

66-67 ATLANTIC OCEAN, SOUTH AFRICA – AN IMPOSING BREAKER THREATENS A GROUP OF FISHERMEN IN THE PORT OF KALK BAY.

68-69 Atlantic Ocean, Spain — A breaker rises to such a height that it towers over the lighthouse on the island of Muro.

70-71 Mediterranean Sea, France — After lifting the foam off the crests of the waves, a powerful gust of wind assails the Marseille lighthouse.

"BE EVER LIKE THE SEA:
EVEN THOUGH IT BREAKS
ITSELF AGAINST THE CLIFFS,
IT ALWAYS FINDS THE
STRENGTH TO TRY AGAIN."

JIM MORRISON

THE BRAVE SAILORS

INTENSE COLD, ADVERSE WEATHER, MEN ARE OFTEN NOT AWARE OF THEIR COURAGE. SEAFARERS ALWAYS LIVE ON THE CUTTING EDGE: EITHER OUT OF NECESSITY—THE CREW OF A DEEP SEA TUG, AN OCEAN LINER IN A STORM, OR THE SOLITARY WORKERS ON OIL PLATFORMS; OR TO SAVE THE LIVES OF OTHERS—THE CREWS OF RESCUE BOATS. IT IS THIS CONTINUAL UNCERTAINTY, SECRET AND DISQUIETING, THAT MAKES THE MEN OF THE SEA SO FASCINATING.

AT SEA, THE SPACES ARE IMMENSE, THE DISTANCES OVERWHELMING, THE SPEEDS ARE RELATIVE, AND NOT COMPARABLE TO THOSE ON LAND, A MERCHANT SHIP CAN REACH 20 KNOTS, ABOUT 25 MPH (40 KM/H), IF WINDS ARE NOT UNFAVORABLE. THE SEA IS HARD, IT CONSTRAINS ALL TO DEAL WITH RHYTHMS, TIMES, AND MANNERS THAT DO NOT BELONG TO IT, AND THIS IS WHY A MAN OF THE SEA WORKS, LIVES, AND STRUGGLES IN A WAY DIFFERENT THAN ALL OTHER CONTEXTS.

THE MEN WHO CROSS THE OCEANS STAY IN GROUPS. THEY SUPPORT ONE ANOTHER, THEY ERASE ALL DIVERSITY, AND THEY ANNUL ALL ARISTOCRACY. AND THE HARDER THE VOYAGE, THE STORMIER THE SEAS, THE HIGHER THE NAUTICAL TEAM SPIRIT RISES TO CHALLENGE THE ADVERSE ELEMENT. AN ELEMENT THAT CAN BE PITILESS, BUT WHICH ALSO CAN GENERATE CAPACITIES FOR PATIENCE AND RESPECT, A SENSE OF LIBERTY; IT'S A BENCH TEST FOR HUMAN VIRTUES, A PLACE WHERE COURAGE, HOPES, AND DREAMS MOVE UNDISTURBED.

THE HOWL OF THE SEA, PRESSED BY THUNDER, LIGHTNING, AND INTENSE PRECIPITATION, HAS CONTINUALLY INSPIRED LITERATURE. TALES OF MEN STRUGGLING AGAINST THE ELEMENTS. THE TALES OF THOSE WHO HAVE LIVED THE SEA GO WASTED IN PORT TAVERNS. "THE WAVES STARTED COMING AT EXCEPTIONALLY SHORT INTERVALS," RECALLS BILLY GAIL, CAPTAIN OF THE *ANDREA GAIL*, A FISHING BOAT THAT WAS CRUISING OFF

THE COAST OF NOVA SCOTIA IN OCTOBER 1991 DURING THE STORM OF THE CENTURY. "INSTEAD OF COMING EVERY 15 SECONDS, THEY WERE COMING EVERY 8 OR 9." THE SHORTER THE INTERVAL, THE STEEPER THE WAVE FRONTS ARE, AND THE GREATER THE POSSIBILITY FOR THEM TO BREAK. A BREAKING WAVE OF 50 FEET (15 METERS) IS MORE DESTRUCTIVE THAN ONE TWICE THAT HEIGHT. "THE ONLY ALTERNATIVE," CONTINUES BILLY, "WAS TO COME ABOUT INTO THE WIND WITH VERY ROUGH SEAS, A MANEUVER THAT ALARMED ME, I FELT ALONE IN THE IMMENSITY. I HAD NO CHOICE." WHEN THE BOAT LEAVES ITSELF OPEN TO TRANSVERSE WAVES, EVEN FOR JUST HALF A MINUTE, IT CAN CAPSIZE. THE PORTHOLES ARE EXPOSED TO THE BREAKERS, THE BOAT CONSUMES MORE FUEL, AND THE AFT TENDS TO TAKE THE WIND, DRAGGING THE CRAFT DOWNWIND. EVEN AIRCRAFT CARRIERS RISK SHIPWRECK WHEN THEY END UP TRANSVERSE WITH THE SEA IN A STORM. "I HAD TO FIND A PAUSE BETWEEN THE WAVES AND COME ABOUT INTO THE WIND, GETTING MYSELF TO THE PROW AT THE RIGHT MOMENT. PURE STRUGGLE FOR SURVIVAL. STANDING AT THE TILLER, I BRACED MYSELF AGAINST THE WORST WITH ALL THE STRENGTH I HAD, HOPING NOT TO TAKE A ROGUE WAVE ON THE SIDE. THE SEA WAS CONFUSED, MOUNTAINS OF WATER WERE CONVERGING, SEPARATING, OVERLAPPING ONE ANOTHER IN ALL DIRECTIONS. THEN SUDDENLY THE STORM ABATED, THE WINDS DROPPED A FEW KNOTS, THE WAVES CALMED, THE PERIODS LENGTHENED, THE BREAKERS BEGAN TO QUIET. I CLIMB UP THE FRONT OF EACH WAVE AND FALL BACK DOWN ALONG ITS BACK, BUT THE ELECTRONIC INSTRUMENTS ARE USELESS AND THE CREW HAS FALLEN PREY TO PANIC. FOR THE FIRST TIME, WE ARE INEXORABLY ALONE IN THE MIDDLE OF THE SEA."

THAT COMBINATION OF OPPOSING FORCES — RAPIDLY SHIFTING HIGH AND LOW PRESSURES — GIVES RISE TO HIGH, CONSTANT WINDS AND GIGANTIC WAVES THAT CAN SINK ANY TYPE OR SIZE OF SHIP. MEN OF THE SEA WORK IN A PARTICULAR ENVIRONMENT, IN A PARTICULAR CONTEXT: MILLIONS OF BILLIONS OF H_2O MOLECULES, AS FAR AS THE EYE CAN SEE.

THE MARINER IS ONE OF THE MOST ANCIENT FIGURES AMONG WORKERS, SINCE NAVIGATION IS ONE OF HUMANITY'S MOST ARCHAIC ARTS. THE FIRST DOCUMENTED SEA VOYAGES DATE BACK TO ANCIENT EGYPT, OVER 5000 YEARS AGO, AND MANY ARE THE TESTIMONIES OF LONG CROSSINGS BY THE PHOENICIANS, THE GREEKS, THE PERSIANS, ROMANS, ARABS, VIKINGS, AND BASQUES. IT TOOK MILLENNIA OF EXPLORATIONS TO PUT TOGETHER THE MAP OF THE GLOBE. EVEN TODAY, THE WORK TAKES PLACE IN SOMETIMES ADVERSE CONDITIONS THAT TRY THE NATURE OF THE INDIVIDUAL.

IN THE COLLECTIVE IMAGERY, FED BY BOOKS AND FILMS, THE HEROIC AGE OF NAVIGATION IS MADE UP OF GREAT COMMANDERS, OCEAN CROSSINGS CONDUCTED AT MAXIMUM SPEED THROUGH STORMS, CARGO SHIPS, PIRATE SHIPS, SCIENTIFIC AND NATURALISTIC VOYAGES. THE PHOTOS OF PORTS FROM THE EARLY 1900S ARE FASCINATING: MYRIADS OF SPARS, MAINMASTS, MEN AT THE QUAY, AND TONS OF WARES. THEY ILLUSTRATE LABOR TENACITY, ACTS OF CIVILITY, MEN, GESTURES, AND AN ENTIRE CULTURE, NOT TO BE FORGOTTEN.

TODAY, THE CHARACTERISTICS AND CONDITIONS OF THE WORK ONBOARD SHIPS AND OIL RIGS HAVE CHANGED DRASTICALLY. IT'S ENOUGH TO REALIZE THAT PERSONNEL CAN REACH THEIR WORK POSTS BY HELICOPTER INSTEAD OF FACING LONG CROSSINGS, AND THAT CONDITIONS OF LIVING ONBOARD ENJOY THE IMPROVEMENTS CONNECTED WITH PROGRESSES IN TECHNOLOGY, MEDICINE, SCIENCE, FOOD SERVICE, AND, ESPECIALLY, COMMUNICATION. MANY JOBS RELATED TO THE SEA HAVE DISAPPEARED, AS IN THE CASE OF THE LEGENDARY LIGHTHOUSE WATCHMAN — THESE DAYS THE WORK IS DONE BY A SIMPLE COMPUTER, OR THOSE WHO STILL EXIST PERFORM THEIR WORK IN SAFER CONDITIONS. AND YET THE OCEANS, WITH THEIR CHARGE OF BEAUTY AND TRAGEDY, ARE TODAY STILL THE ANARCHIC, UNCONTROLLABLE TERRITORY OF STORMS, WHERE SCIENCE AND REASON ENCOUNTER THE LAWS OF CHAOS, AND GENERATE LEGENDS.

76-77 North Sea, Iceland – An English fishing boat challenges the fury of the stormy sea.

78-79 Atlantic Ocean, France – Waves overcoming the tug's gunwale during a storm.

"WHEN MEN COME TO THE
POINT THAT THEY ARE SATISFIED
WITH LIFE AT SEA, THEY ARE
NO LONGER SUITED FOR LIVING
ON TERRA FIRMA."

SAMUEL JOHNSON

80-81 AND 82-83 ATLANTIC OCEAN, FRANCE – TUGS FACE THE WORST
POSSIBLE WEATHER CONDITIONS IN ORDER TO TOW SHIPS TO SAFETY. WAVES
ASSAILING THE BRIDGE DURING MANEUVERS CONSTITUTE AN ADDITIONAL
DANGER TO SEAMEN.

"AFTER THAT MAGIC INSTANT WHEN MY
EYES WERE OPENED IN THE SEA, IT WAS
NO LONGER POSSIBLE FOR ME TO SEE,
TO THINK, TO LIVE, AS BEFORE."

JACQUES-YVES COUSTEAU

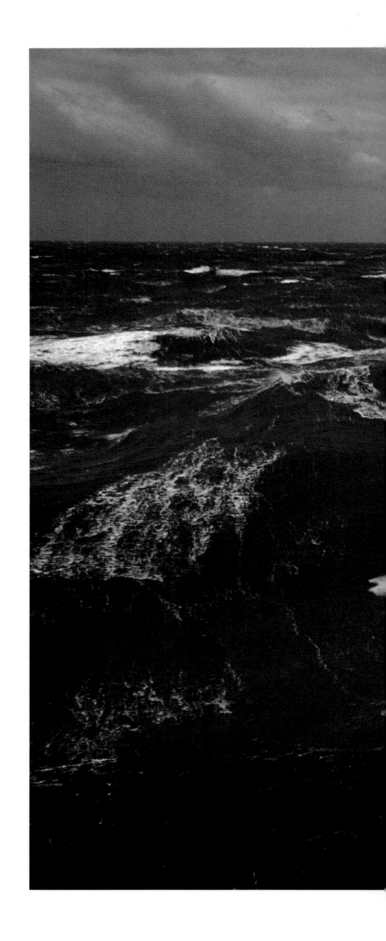

84-85 AND 86-87 BERING SEA, ALASKA, U.S. – THE PROHIBITIVE WORKING CONDITIONS ON BOARD FISHING SHIPS ARE MADE EVEN MORE DIFFICULT BY AN IMPETUOUS STORM OBLIGING THESE CRAMP FISHERMEN TO BRAVE WINDS OF OVER 50 KNOTS.

"FISHERMEN KNOW THAT THE SEA IS DANGEROUS AND THAT THE TEMPESTS ARE TERRIBLE, BUT THEY HAVE NEVER CONSIDERED THOSE DANGERS TO BE SUFFICIENT REASON FOR REMAINING ON DRY LAND."

VINCENT VAN GOGH

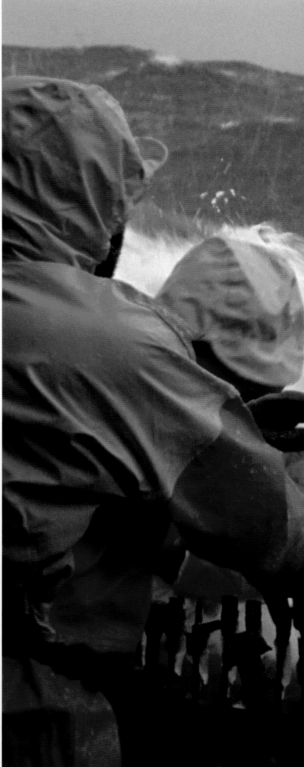

88-89 North Sea – A team of Spanish fishermen brave the force 9 ocean waves.

90-91 Drake's Canal, Antarctica – The prow of a passenger ship defies the high waves characteristic of this narrow sea passage.

"Then all collapsed,
and the great shroud of the
sea rolled on as it rolled
five thousand years ago."

Herman Melville
Moby Dick

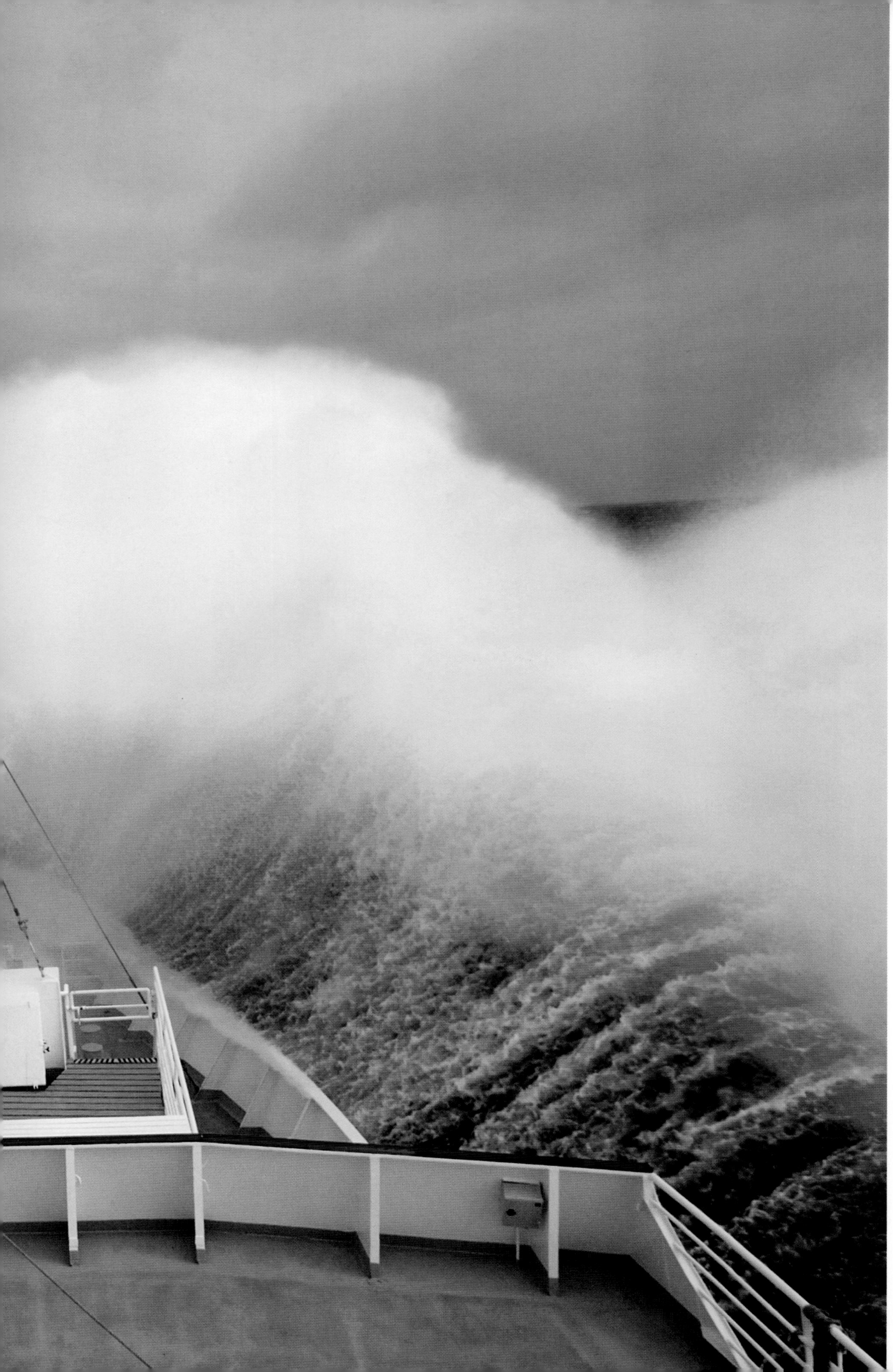

92-93 PACIFIC OCEAN, WASHINGTON, U.S. – A COAST GUARD PATROL SHIP FACES AN IMPOSING WALL OF FOAM GENERATED BY THE WAVES BREAKING ON THE SHORE.

94-95 Pacific Ocean, Washington, U.S. – In winter, a tract of coast facing the mouth of the Columbia River is struck by waves as high as 23 ft (7 m).

96 ATLANTIC OCEAN, FRANCE – WINTER TEMPESTS OFF THE COAST OF BELLE-ÎLE REPRESENT THE GREATEST CHALLENGE FOR COAST GUARD VESSELS.

97 Atlantic Ocean, France – Assisting swimmers in trouble off the coasts of France is the duty of the French national society for sea rescue (Société Nationale de Sauvetage en Mer: SNSM).

98-99 ATLANTIC OCEAN, FRANCE — ENORMOUS WAVES OVERPOWER A PATROL BOAT OF THE SNSM OFF THE BRITTANY COAST.

100-101 ATLANTIC OCEAN, FRANCE – THE CREW OF A COAST GUARD SHIP CHALLENGES THE WAVES UNLEASHED BY A VIOLENT ATLANTIC STORM.

102-103 BEARING SEA, ALASKA, U.S. – HEEDLESS OF THE WAVES PASSING OVER THE GUNWALE, THE CREW OF A FISHING BOAT CONTINUE ON WITH THEIR WORK ON THE SHIP'S BRIDGE.

104-105 ATLANTIC OCEAN, FRANCE – ON THE UNSTABLE TRACT OF SEA
ALONG THE COAST OF BRITTANY, STORMS CAPABLE OF TREMENDOUS
VIOLENCE ARE GENERATED, WITH WAVES AS HIGH AS 23 FT (7 M).

106-107 AND 108-109 ATLANTIC OCEAN, ICELAND – A NIGHT STORM BESETS A FISHING BOAT OFF THE COAST OF ICELAND, PUTTING THE CREW TO A HARD TEST, AND MAKING VISIBILITY ALMOST NIL.

"While you're looking at it, you do not notice how much noise it makes. But in the darkness... all that infinity becomes merely uproar, a wall of sound, a blind, harassing howl. You do not extinguish it, the sea, when it burns in the night."

Alessandro Baricco

110-111 Bering Sea, Alaska, U.S. – The forceful storm winds add further difficulty to the long operations of bringing in the nets.

112-113 Atlantic Ocean, Norway – An imposing oiler resembles a toy at the mercy of the ocean waves.

WAVES

"Every wave knows it is the sea. What undoes it does not disturb it, because what breaks it creates it anew." (Lao Tse)

In a storm, between the motions of the waves and terra firma, an ambiguous relationship is created, unpredictable and uncontrollable, frightful. They flog it with ferocious violence, and then just barely lap at it. While lightning and thunder shatter the sky, they erode the shore with force and spite until it completely changes appearance. Wedging themselves among the rocky ravines, the waves dampen and break up their impetus, causing spouts and depressions in the air, or they break, and with power unheard, they carry stones and sand in a perpetual motion. The sea storm is the ultimate expression of the force of nature: mighty waves driven by the winds, or the rumble of the waves with foamy white crests that follow one another, as in mad assault, toward the coast. They arrive from afar, charged with force, ever unique and ever diverse. There are places where the breakers arrive after a journey of 1800-2500 miles (3000-4000 km), like the Hawaiian Islands, with a bottom that suddenly rises from a depth of 23,000 ft (7000 m) and the waters scale the walls of volcanoes, arriving almost to the sky. Here we understand the preponderance of the stormy sea: when waves have the force of throwing you to the ground and dragging you away.

In other places, the oceans meet and waves are weapons with which they compete, as at Cape Horn. You need to witness it to understand the tumult of the waves: labyrinths of water that

Transcend the force of gravity, they rise in looming walls and open into bottomless abysses of legends and nightmares. The wind, which, far off the coast, can make itself felt even in the depths, impresses character on the water's surface, giving it vigor, energy, and a fury almost aggressive. There's no respite, no pause.

The dimensions of the waves are connected not only to the source generating them, but also to the size of the basin in which they form. In the great blue of the oceans, the waves reach dizzying heights, over 50-65 feet (15-20 meters), without speaking of rogue waves, mysterious and unpredictable, reaching peaks of 80-100 feet (25-30 meters) in height. When the wave encounters an obstacle, it can rise well over these dimensions, as in the turbulent waters at the Cape of Good Hope. Reached for the first time by Portuguese navigator Vasco de Gama in 1497, it was christened with that name of good omen because it was the southernmost point in circumnavigating Africa. It was a grand celebration on the vessels of times past when the yet distant, confused outline of a promontory promised that soon they would be rounding the Cape. And once having arrived there, there was the hope that the voyage would become easier, less dangerous. For the first navigators coming from Europe, this was the crux. Countless are the legends and stories, many of them true, telling of the terrible storms characterizing the embrace between the Atlantic and the Indian Oceans. The waters were infested with ghost ships and frightful monsters. Like Adamastor, the horrible giant who, for having surprised a nymph while bathing, was transformed by Zeus into the peninsula of the Cape.

Storm waves are capable of wounding the largest, most modern ships; ferocious and scathing, the foam claws mercilessly. Lives suspended between great fortune and deadly risks, and it's the fury of the waves that moves the balancing needle. Like being onboard a sailing ship during a squall: the bowman is working forward, the boat is making leeway, and the splashes start coming. The waves rise, the crests are broken, and the wind vaporizes the tops. The sea is all white, it's bellowing, the stays are whistling. You can't go on with the bowline, the sea won't allow it, it's become an unfair fight, and the strikes to the prow are forceful. They slow you down, you don't go anywhere. The command goes out: we change direction, three hands of reef and tassel, little sail to proceed to the wide slack, but even this is too much. The sad tales of the Fastnet Race, the regatta for deep sea vessels, come to mind. In 1979, several people were killed by the terrible storm that overcame all the boats in the competition. Breakers still, as a collective, represent a semantic universe of emotional significances; they do not represent merely the powerful energy and the changing humors of the sea, but also those of the human spirit.

"The boy felt that a perfect accord existed between himself and that opulence of the surrounding nature. He drew a deep breath, and it was as though a part of that invisible which constitutes nature had permeated the intimacy of his being. He felt the rumble of the waves breaking on the beach, and it was as though the beating of his young blood were synchronized with the movement of the great tides." Yukio Mishima, The Sound of Waves.

As a free man I will ever love the sea!
The sea is your mirror:
you contemplate
Your soul in the infinite turning
of the rolling wave and your spirit
Is an abyss equally bitter.

Charles Baudelaire

118-119 AND 120-121 PACIFIC OCEAN – IMPOSING SURGES BREAK, TRANSFORMING THE OCEAN'S VIBRANT FORCE INTO A RAGING WALL OF WHITE FOAM.

122-123 PACIFIC OCEAN, OREGON, U.S. – THE OCEAN TEMPESTS UNLEASHED OFF THE COAST OF CAPE KIWANDA GIVE RISE TO VIOLENT SEA STORMS.

124-125 PACIFIC OCEAN, HAWAII, U.S. – DURING THE WINTER SEASON, THE COLOSSAL HAWAIIAN WAVES CAN REACH 50 FT (15 M) IN HEIGHT.

"ONE COULD HEAR THE SEA, LIKE A CONTINUAL SNOW SLIDE, THE INCESSANT THUNDER OF A STORM BORN FROM WHO KNOWS WHICH HEAVEN. IT DID NOT CEASE FOR A MOMENT. IT KNEW NO WEARINESS. IT KNEW NO CLEMENCY."

ALESSANDRO BARICCO

126-127 INDIAN OCEAN, MADAGASCAR – THE EXPLOSIVE IMPETUS OF THE SEA STORM CRASHES DOWN ON THE BEACHES OF CAP SAINTE-MARIE.

128-129 PACIFIC OCEAN – EVEN THOUGH THE STORM HAS PASSED, THE FORCEFUL WAVES GENERATED STILL CRASH VIOLENTLY AGAINST THE COASTS.

130-131 Pacific Ocean, Hawaii, U.S. – An ocean wave closes in upon itself, creating a tunnel of crystalline water and giving life to the "perfect wave."

132-133 Pacific Ocean, Hawaii, U.S. – Long waves overlap and break, off the coast of Oahu.

134-135 PACIFIC OCEAN, AUSTRALIA – WHEN THE OCEAN'S IRE REACHES THE COAST, IT CONVERTS INTO A SEQUENCE OF SPECTACULAR ROLLERS.

138-139 PACIFIC OCEAN – THE BROAD FRONT OF THE WAVE RISES, GROWS, AND CURLS BEFORE BREAKING WITH A RUMBLE ONTO THE BEACH.

RIDING THE WAVES

STORM ARRIVING, WIND TENSE, BOWLINE TAUT. WE DECIDE TO KEEP OUR DISTANCE FROM THE COAST. THE SKY IS TURNING GLOOMY. THE SEA KEEPS RISING. IT ROLLS, THE WAVES ARE HIGH, THE CRESTS BREAK UP, AND SUDDEN SPLASHES HIT THE FACE. IT IS NIGHT, BUT THERE ARE NO STARS. WHAT IS AROUND US IS HELL; THESE ARE THE MONSTERS THAT SAILORS IMAGINE. WE CALCULATE THAT THE GUSTS REACH 40 KNOTS. ALL WE HAVE UP IS THE STORM SAIL, WE'RE TAKING WIND AT THE STERN, AND WE'RE STARTING TO SUBMERGE WITH EACH STRIKE OF THE SEA. THE BOAT IS AN ELVSTRØM, VERY SPARTAN, DESIGNED BY A DANE FAMOUS FOR THE NUMBER OF TIMES HE'S PARTICIPATED IN THE OLYMPICS. IT'S A 30-FOOTER (ABOUT 9 METERS) VERY STURDY, FOR THE OCEAN, BUT IN THE STORM, IT'S A SHELL. WE MANAGE TO HANDLE IT WELL; THE RIGGING, MAST, AND HALYARDS ARE HOLDING UP MAGNIFICENTLY. WE SAIL WITH SEA BEHIND US, THE WAVES ARE SO HIGH THEY BREAK ON THE STERN, INVADE THE WELL DECK, THEY COLLAPSE ON MY BACK AND LITERALLY SHOVE ME FORWARD, KNOCK ME AGAINST THE COMPASS. I HIT IT WITH MY FACE AND TURN AROUND. I DON'T SEE ANYTHING CLEARLY BUT CAN PERCEIVE WHAT LIFTED ME. IT'S NOTHING HUMAN. IT'S WATER, LOTS OF WATER. WE PUT ON THE SAFETY BELTS, A TYPE OF VEST WITH STEEL CABLE AND SNAP RING, NEEDED NOW MORE THAN EVER! THE VANES OF THE WIND-GENERATOR WHISTLE LOUDLY, CONSTANTLY, GIVING LARGE AMOUNTS OF CURRENT: THE SAILING LIGHTS, COMPASS LIGHTS, WELL DECK LIGHTS, ALL SHINE BRILLIANTLY.

MY FRIEND AND I HAVE TO SHOUT TO HEAR EACH OTHER. WE RELIEVE EACH OTHER AT THE HELM SO WE CAN EAT SOMETHING. WHEN I GO BELOW, I REALIZE WHAT MONSTER IT IS THAT'S BEATING US: EVERYTHING IS FLYING ABOUT, I HAVE TO BRACE MY ARMS AND LEGS TO KEEP MYSELF STANDING, BUT I'M NOT ABLE TO EAT.

I BRACE MYSELF FORCEFULLY BETWEEN THE WRITING TABLE AND THE KITCHEN AND SWALLOW SOMETHING. I HEAR LOUD NOISES AND TREMENDOUS BLOWS, THEN STRONG ACCELERATION AND AN INFERNAL NOISE COMING FROM OUTSIDE, ALARMING, YES, FRIGHTENING. I GO BACK ON DECK. MY FRIEND IS AT THE HELM, COMPLETELY DRENCHED, THE OILCLOTH DIDN'T HOLD, AND MEANWHILE THE SEA IS STRIKING EVER HARDER. WE'RE IN THE TEMPEST. HE SHOUTS IN MY EAR: "SEA FORCE 7 AND WIND FORCE 8!" I TAKE THE HELM AND HE GOES BELOW TO DRY OFF AND EAT SOMETHING. AFTER A BIT, HE CONFIRMS THE ROUTE I HAVE TO FOLLOW. I NO LONGER LOOK AT THE COMPASS, I KEEP THE SEA AT THE AFT QUARTER OR AT THE STERN, WIND ASTERN, AND WE MOVE AHEAD. STRAIGHT AHEAD OF ME A FEW CLOUDS HAVE LEFT AN OPENING THROUGH WHICH I SEE A SMALL STAR, I DON'T KNOW WHICH ONE, BUT I USE IT TO HOLD THE ROUTE, IT'S TO THE SOUTH AND THAT'S ALL I NEED, I POINT THE BOW AT THE STAR.

IT ALL CONTINUES ON SO VERY VIOLENTLY, IT WON'T CALM, AND NOW IT'S BEEN 14 HOURS WE'VE BEEN TOTTERING ALONG. I DON'T FEEL TIRED, BUT I'M AFRAID SOMETHING MIGHT BREAK, I'M AFRAID A STAY MIGHT GIVE AND THE MAST MIGHT BREAK; WE'D SINK IN 30 SECONDS! I DON'T LOOK BACK, I THINK ONLY OF STEERING. NOW IT'S AT ITS GREATEST, EACH WAVE IS A STRIKE, WE'RE LITERALLY COVERED BY THE SEA, FROM STERN TO PROW, THE WELL DECK FILLS WITH WATER UP TO OUR KNEES, IT SWIFTLY FLOWS AWAY, AND THEN IT STARTS AGAIN. I BRACE MY LEGS WELL, AND WITH ONE HAND I HOLD ON TO THE RUNNERS, THE OTHER STEADY ON THE RUDDER, AND RIGHT THEN, IN THAT MOMENT, I FEEL THE STERN RISING, OUT OF THE WATER, THE RUDDER WON'T STEER, AND THE BOAT, LIKE A TORPEDO, RUNS ON THE WAVE THAT RISES GRADUALLY, LIFTING US TO SURF OUT OF CONTROL, SMASHING THE WHOLE PROW INTO THE HOLLOW OF THE WAVE. I ACKNOWLEDGE THE BLOW, AND THE NEXT

WAVE; WITH BOAT STEADY, IT COVERS US COMPLETELY. WE FEAR FOR THE STAYS AND THE SAFETY OF THE MAST: THAT'S THE GREAT WORRY, WHILE ALL AROUND IS WAVES, FOAM, AND WIND.

WE'RE WORN OUT, BOTH OF US, WE'VE ALTERNATED AT THE HELM FOR HOURS, AND WE CAN'T DO ANYTHING OTHER THAN SAIL WITH THE WIND ASTERN. EVERY ONCE IN A WHILE MY FRIEND LOOKS AT THE LOG. HE TELLS ME THAT WHILE COASTING WE HIT 11 KNOTS! INCREDIBLE! IT'S LIKE A FIAT 500 HITTING 125 MILES (200 KM) AN HOUR! WE'VE GONE MANY MILES, ALWAYS KEEPING AWAY FROM THE COAST. NOW IT'S DAY AND WE CAN SEE WHAT'S AROUND US, A TIMID SUN IS RISING, AND FOR THE FIRST TIME, I HEAR THE WIND-GENERATOR STOPPING, AT TIMES ITS WHISTLING…THE WIND IS DROPPING. NOW I TURN BACKWARD AND I'M ABLE TO STEER MORE EASILY. MY FRIEND, A GREAT HELMSMAN AND SAILOR, RELIEVES ME AT THE RUDDER, AND SAYD ME HE THINKS WE CAN TRY PUTTING UP THE MAINSAIL, JUST ONE HAND. MORE AND MORE, AS THE HOURS MOVE ALONG, THE SEA IS CALMING DOWN. WE'VE BEEN SAILING WITHOUT SIGHT OF LAND FOR NEARLY TWO DAYS, AND THE SUN IS SETTING. TOWARD EVENING WE PULL THEM ALL UP, NOW THAT WE CAN, WE START UP THE AUTOMATIC RUDDER, AND EAT. WE LIE DOWN ON DECK AND FOR THE FIRST TIME, WE LET OURSELVES GO, INVOLUNTARILY, INTO A LIGHT MOOD, THE ONLY ONE UP TO NOW: WE COLLAPSE, LITERALLY, INTO SLEEP, BOTH OF US, WITH OUR BOOTS STILL ON, SAFETY BELTS ABANDONED IN THE WELL DECK, THE BOAT FLOATING ALONG. THE BEATING OF THE SAILS IN A LIGHT BREEZE AWAKENS US AT DAWN, THE BOAT PROCEEDING SLOWLY ALONG WITH THE DRONE OF THE AUTOMATIC RUDDER AS IT GIVES ITS SLIGHT CORRECTIONS TO THE ROUTE. THE WORST HAS PASSED. BY EVENING WE'LL BE AT OUR DESTINATION.

144-145 PACIFIC OCEAN, AUSTRALIA – THE OCEAN'S DIFFICULT CONDITIONS PUT THE *SKANDIA*'S CREW TO A RIGOROUS TRIAL.

146-147 ATLANTIC OCEAN, ANTIGUA – ABOARD THE *ASHANTI IV*, A WAVE SUBMERGES SAILORS WITH FOAM DURING THE ANNUAL REGATTA OFF THE COAST OF ANTIGUA.

"One needs to free oneself from the hope that the sea might ever rest. We must learn to navigate in strong winds."

Aristotele Onassis

148-149 Atlantic Ocean, France – The *Commodore* faces the difficult beginning of the Jules Verne Trophy Race.

150-151 Atlantic Ocean, France – Extreme weather conditions do not stop the clip of the trimaran *Fujicolor* during the Brest Multihull Grand Prix.

152-153 Pacific Ocean – Skipper Sébastien Josse resists the fury of an ocean storm single-handedly, as provided for by the rules of the Vendée Globe regatta.

154-155 Southern Pacific Ocean – Trimming the sails during a storm proves to be not only a dangerous challenge for the crew but also extremely tiring.

156-157 Atlantic Ocean – During the Figaro Transat crossing, the prow of the *Brit Air* plunges surely through the waves.

158-159 ATLANTIC OCEAN, FRANCE – THE *SODEBO* CHALLENGES THE OCEAN'S FURIOUS WATERS DURING THE TRANSAT JACQUES VABRE.

160-161 Pacific Ocean, California, U.S. – A cloudburst raging over San Francisco Bay makes bridgework dangerous and exhausting.

162-163 Atlantic Ocean, France – Winds blowing at over 40 knots and high ocean waves put the yacht to a hard test during the Figaro Transat.

164-165 ATLANTIC OCEAN, ANTIGUA – IN A BAY OFF ANTIGUA, THE *WINDROSE*'S ELEGANT SAILS STRETCH AND FILL UNDER PRESSURE OF RISING WINDS.

166-167 ATLANTIC OCEAN – FRENCH SKIPPER THOMAS ROUXEL CHALLENGES WAVES THAT OVERWHELM THE HULL OF THE YACHT, SUBMERGING IT WITH FOAM.

168-169 ATLANTIC OCEAN – A SUDDEN SQUALL SURPRISES THE *ASTRA*, PUTTING THE CREW'S SAFETY AT RISK.

170-171 ATLANTIC OCEAN, FRANCE – JUST A FEW MINUTES AFTER STARTING OFF ON THE TRANSAT JACQUES VABRE, GIOVANNI SOLDINI AND VITTO MALINGRI'S CATAMARAN FACES THE FIRST OCEAN STORM.

172-173 Pacific Ocean – The women's crew of the *Amer Sports* strives to control the boat amidst the breakers during the transatlantic leg of the Volvo Ocean Race.

174-175 Pacific Ocean – Ocean crossings constitute an extremely tough bench test, not only for vessels, but also for mariners, alone at the mercy of the ocean's might.

176-177 Pacific Ocean, Chile – The *Sariyah* challenges the legendary storms off Cape Horn.

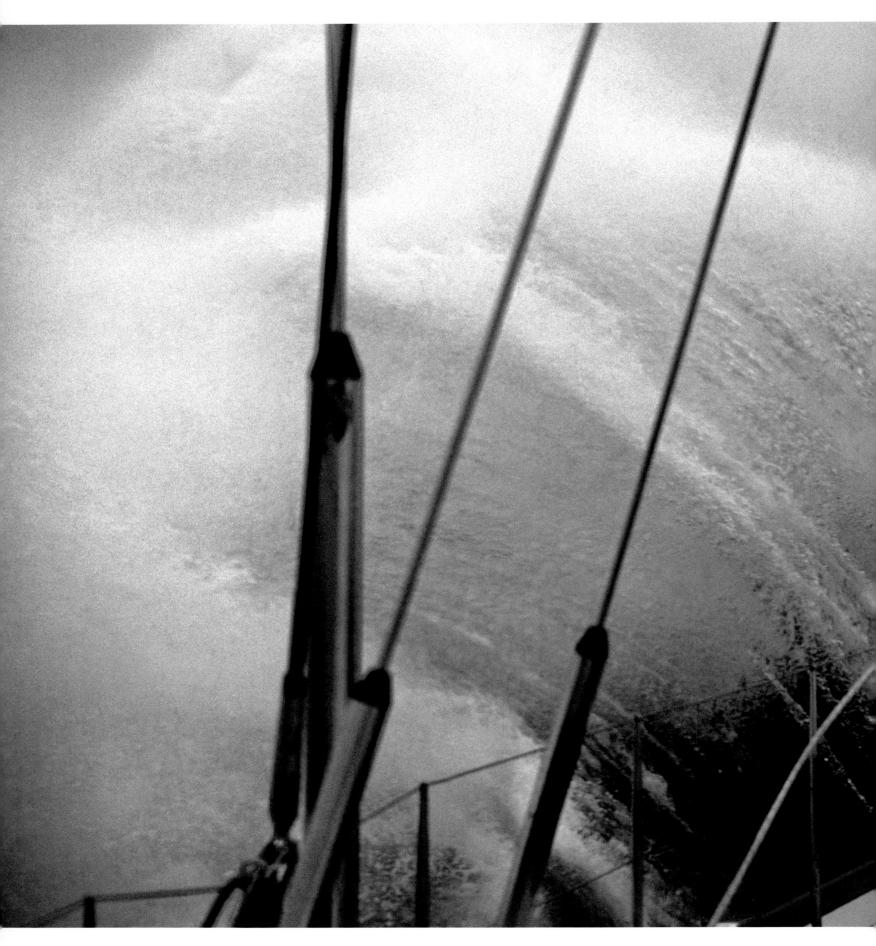

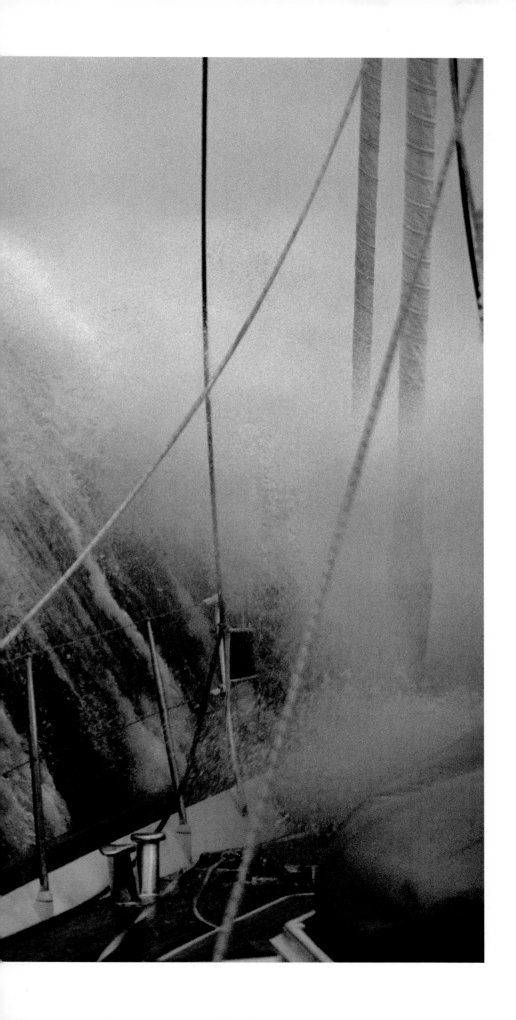

"MARINERS KNOW THAT ONE
DOES NOT GOVERN THE SEA,
THAT ONE MANEUVERS THE
SAILS, AND NOT THE WINDS."

GIULIO TREMONTI

178-179 Atlantic Ocean – The multihull *Fujifilm* advances by gliding over the crests of the waves.

180-181 ATLANTIC OCEAN – THE *GROUPAMA*'S HULL, OVER 60 FT (18 M) LONG, DISAPPEARS BENEATH A BROAD WAVE THAT OVERTAKES IT.

182-183 ATLANTIC OCEAN – THE PROW OF THE LARGE TRIMARAN *BANQUE POPULAIRE* PLUNGES WITHOUT HESITATION INTO THE CREST OF A WAVE.

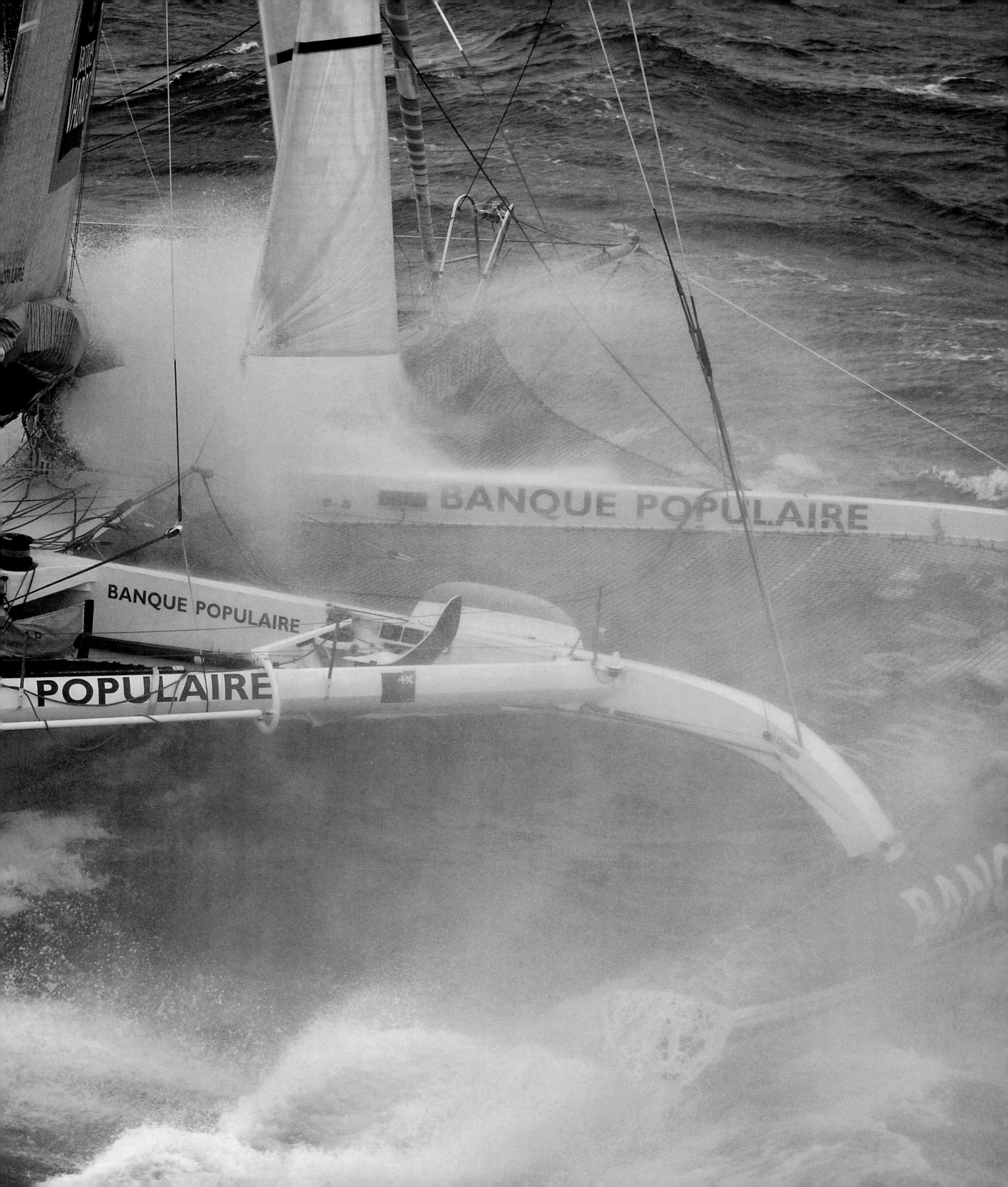
BANQUE POPULAIRE
BANQUE POPULAIRE
POPULAIRE

184-185 ATLANTIC OCEAN, IRELAND – FOAM FROM THE WAVES, DRAGGED BY WINDS EXCEEDING 30 KNOTS, OVERTAKES THE PROW OF A YACHT COMPETING IN THE VOLVO OCEAN RACE.

186-187 ATLANTIC OCEAN – SKIPPER GIOVANNI SOLDINI TRIMS THE MAINSAIL OF THE MULTIHULL *TIM PROGETTO ITALIA* TO WITHSTAND ADVERSE WEATHER CONDITIONS DURING THE TRANSAT JACQUES VABRE.

188-189 ATLANTIC OCEAN – AS IT GLIDES OVER THE CRESTS OF THE WAVES, THE MULTIHULL *FONCIA* SEEMS IT COULD TAKE FLIGHT.

190-191 Pacific Ocean, Hawaii, U.S. – After a storm, a windsurfer ventures amid the swells at Hookipa Beach.

192-193 Pacific Ocean, Hawaii, U.S. – The sea storm unleashed off the coasts of Maui is an occasion not to be missed for daredevil windsurfers.

194-195 Pacific Ocean – Surrounded by a sea of white foam, the sailing boat seems almost to be gliding among the clouds.

196-197 Pacific Ocean, Hawaii, U.S. – A surfer awaits the arrival of the "perfect wave" at Hookipa Beach.

198-199 Pacific Ocean – Desire to compete against one's own limits and to dominate the uncontrollable force of the sea drives lovers of the surf to challenge waves higher than 13 ft (4 m).

"THE SEA HAS NEVER BEEN A FRIEND
TO MAN. AT THE MOST, IT IS AN
ACCOMPLICE TO HIS RESTLESSNESS."

JOSEPH CONRAD

200-201 PACIFIC OCEAN, HAWAII, U.S. – SURFER GARRETT MCNAMARA PASSING THROUGH A TUBE: AN EPHEMERAL *TUNNEL* FORMED BY A WAVE CLOSING IN UPON ITSELF.

202-203 Pacific Ocean, Hawaii, U.S. – A helicopter utilized in filming surfers' evolutions confronts the wall of foam generated by rollers off Maui.

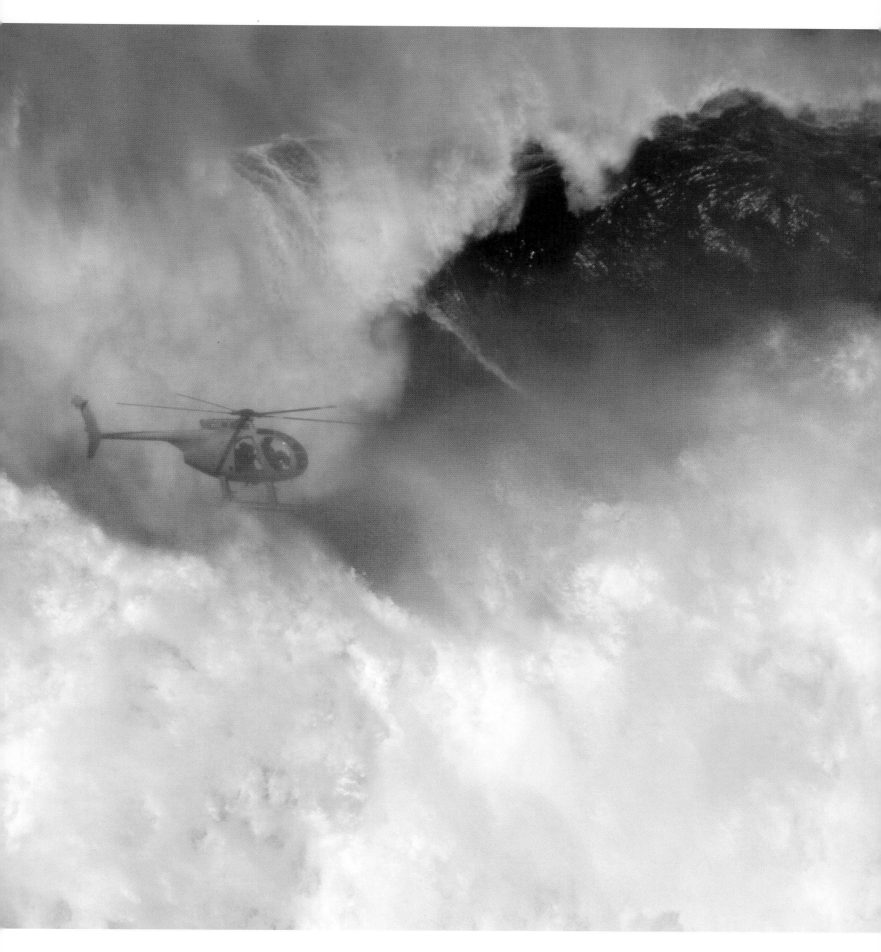

204-205 AND 206-207 PACIFIC OCEAN, HAWAII, U.S. – DUE TO THEIR DANGER, LOCALS CALL THEM *JAWS*, AFTER THE FILM, BUT FAR FROM BEING FRIGHTFUL, THE WAVES THAT BREAK AT PEAHI TO THE NORTH OF MAUI ATTRACT THE WORLD'S BEST SURFERS, COMMITTED TO CHALLENGING THEIR DIMENSIONS AND RENOWN.